UNSEEN
UNTOLD
IS
UNSOLD

UNSEEN UNTOLD I$ UNSOLD

Salesmanship & Common Sense

By
Donald E. Hults

Order this book online at www.trafford.com
or email orders@trafford.com

Most Trafford titles are also available at major online book retailers.

© Copyright 2009 Donald E. Hults.
Design by Ashley Sherrow
First Edition

Note for Librarians: A cataloguing record for this book is available from Library and Archives Canada at www.collectionscanada.ca/amicus/index-e.html

Printed in Victoria, BC, Canada.

ISBN: 978-1-4269-1883-4 (soft)
ISBN: 978-1-4269-1884-1 (hard)

Library of Congress Control Number: 2009936936

Our mission is to efficiently provide the world's finest, most comprehensive book publishing service, enabling every author to experience success. To find out how to publish your book, your way, and have it available worldwide, visit us online at www.trafford.com

Trafford rev. 10/13/2009

 www.trafford.com

North America & international
toll-free: 1 888 232 4444 (USA & Canada)
phone: 250 383 6864 ♦ fax: 812 355 4082

*Dedicated to my wife Ruth for putting-up with me
for these many years, correcting my spelling, proofreading
and still loving me in spite of it all.*

Sales People of the World
Be Proud!

Small business in the USA is the backbone of our economy. So-called "Small Business" is in fact very big business and makes it possible for the giant corporations to exist. They can't do it without you. There are a thousand small businesses out there for every giant corporation and it is those small businesses that need to buy your stuff. This is where you, the sales person is indispensable. If anyone demeans your job as a salesperson, you can be sure they have no idea what keeps business in business. No company can sustain itself without sales. Nothing happens until someone buys something. Being a sales person for one of these "Small Businesses" is what this book is about. Be Proud.

Contents

Opening Comments

When you made the decision to be in sales, did you realize you were about to enter a world of triumph and disappointment, winning and loosing? Neither did I. If you are in this interesting career you have discovered the rewards and frustrations. If you are about to join this distinguished group, you will find out and in the process pay your dues. The basic idea in this little book is to inform the beginner that there are rules to the game, and remind the experienced about some skills you may have forgotten. As for the veteran entrepreneur you will find a few revelations to add to your bag of tricks and in addition to this there are motivating anecdotes, instructions and reminders. Common sense is good salesmanship. It is how we make intelligent choices. Common sense is the adhesive that helps us make smart decisions. Making good decisions is a course of action not done on impulse. It is an indispensable part of this book.

Reading this book may help you change how you live your life. It can help you make more money. The main purpose is to bring you new ideas and to put your feet squarely back on solid ground of selling basics and to start using them again. Consider this a tool box of reminders. You may find some power tools to help get work completed more quickly.

Being in sales is the only career where you meet outstanding people in all walks of life and make new friends. You will also meet your share of disagreeable people, known as customers from hell who can, believer-it-or- not, become your "best customers". Don't rush to judgment about anyone. As a final point, occasionally expect ungentlemanly conduct from your competition.

In preparing to write this book I have done a bit of research about self help books. I have investigated the shelves at Barnes & Noble, Borders and others to discover recent volumes on the subject of salesmanship and motivation. The problem with many seemed to be a lot of word padding without getting to the meat of the subject quickly. This book has no padding, gimmicks or devices, just good salesmanship habits and lots of stuff about common sense and structures you can use to survive in the business of selling and personal relationships in your life. I won't waste your time.

1
Why I Became a Salesman

I was in the commercial photography business for 50 years. It became more successful when I stopped doing the actual photography and used my time for selling and servicing customers. The reason I did this was fear that the first successful sales person I hired would blackmail me into making them a partner. Being a control freak I could not let that happen. So, I became the salesman and sales manager for several years until the business increased so I could hire sales people. There is safety in numbers.

The main business was photographing products that could be printed in color catalogs for use by manufacturers and importers. In addition to the photography studio we eventually put together an art department for layout and design of the catalogs. We outsourced and took responsibility for the printing and delivery of the finished catalog. Our busy clients valued this one-stop service.

After fifty years I retired and sold the business. Wishing I had received a lot of this advice early in my career and knowing that vanity and pride are life's biggest thieves, I gladly pass along these rules and ideas that worked for me.

2
How I Earned My Diploma in Sales

Like most of you, I learned selling the hard way. When one thing didn't work I tried something else. When I was eighteen I found a paperback book for 50 cents that changed my life. The title was "How to Win Friends and Influence People" by Dale Carnegie. Where I went that book went, in the Army as a photographer in Japan after WW2, at college and when I started a photography business in New Jersey in 1948. I still have a copy of that book in my library. A few years after starting the business I found another book by Elmer Wheeler titled "How to sell yourself to others". Attending work shops and lectures over the years have helped but nothing beats the very basic drive and desire to succeed.

In 1948 at twenty three years of age, I bought a small portrait studio in East Orange, NJ. You have to start someplace. I replaced what little apparatus the former owner possessed with new lighting equipment that worked. The old sink in the darkroom was half of a WW2 gas tank from a fighter plane. It was replaced with a new stainless steel sink. Also I bought a new lens and view camera that required 8x10 inch film. You can't do quality work without proper tools. I hired a high school student to help out in the darkroom and answer the phone while I did location photography and knocked on doors.

At this time of my life I didn't have goals, I had ambition. I wanted to be the biggest and best commercial photography company in the USA. That wasn't a bad goal, but it lacked a plan. I disliked photographing babies and weddings so I did everything I could to get as much commercial work as possible. At that time, that was a plan.

By 1950 I photographed my last wedding. You just don't build a commercial photography business without commercial customers. I needed

We got lucky and picked up some great accounts like GE, Westing-house, and Edison but I soon leaned that it was the smaller accounts you never heard of, the little companies that came back to you year-in and year-out. They were our bread & butter and they paid the rent.

The business grew and we hired people. Soon, the first studio was too small. In 1954 we purchased property and built a 3000 sq ft. studio with air-conditioning, AC was a big deal then. We always had clients present in the studio when we did their photography. Winter or sum-mer the lights we used made the studio very warm and the air condi-tioning made things comfortable for the customers and staff.

In 1955 the realization hit me that we needed a "product" to sell. Color photography and color printing had become the craze with advertisers, so we added color post cards to our menu of services. They were printed by Dexter Press in Nyack, N.Y. and sold at an affordable price. Here is what we did to obtain that business. We col-lected phone books from the area and copied the addresses of res-taurant and motels and hotels. Dexter sold us 500 sample cards that we put together with a letter and prices then mailed them. That got us started in the post card business. We added manufacturers to the post card mailings list and got more business. The yellow pages were the toughest way to find prospects.

In those early days there were no organized ways of finding prospects. Local chambers of commerce helped a little with names, but getting good information was labor intensive. In 1956 a company that did mass mailings found us and introduced us to an industrial directory of NJ. It opened up big possibilities and opportunities for us; with the help of the mailing house we put together a mailing list of 2000 prospects. The mailing house printed our messages, inserted samples, a business reply card and took it to the post office. That was great. All we had to do now was wait for those reply cards to come flying back. We usually got four to eight. That is a low response rate, BUT of that number we would have two or three new customers who turned out to be steady year after year. We would loose customers occasionally for the usual reason, but that is business.

With interesting ideas in photography we were able to do a better

other states that were less expensive. No one ever complains about saving money. In those early years new technologies happened rapidly in photography and printing and that helped us advance in the graphics industry. Having said all this, it comes down to paying attention to your total business environment. Keeping up with all the new stuff that affects your business.

Selling is usually a battle of wits involving two people trying to give and or get the best deal they can. This is all very basic stuff. Even if you have been in the selling game for years, you may welcome a little tune-up. For starters here are some basics to merge into your sales personality.

3
Here are the Rules of the Game

- Listen More Talk Less. Repeat this to yourself every day.

- The most important words in any language. Please & Thank You.

- Never knock your competition or another person. You belittle yourself.

- Don't lie or make promises you can't keep. It's like shooting yourself in the foot.

- Don't look at your watch or act like you are in a hurry. Go to the bathroom before the meeting.

- Never touch anything on your prospect or customers desk. But, you can look. Learn to read upside down.

- No liquor at lunch. It will follow you the rest of the day.

- Do not wear cologne or perfume. Unless you are looking for a date.

- Refrain from wise cracks and off color jokes. Makes you look like a jerk.

- Never suggest or offer kick-backs, bribes or presents. It can end your career.

- Emphasize the positive. Eliminate the negative.

- Dress for business, not for a night out. Forget the cuff links unless you are a banker or stock broker.

- Never react to rudeness. Respond and be polite- suck it in.

- Never argue. You may win but you'll loose. Bite your tongue.

4
Little Stuff About Etiquette
(you may not need to read this)

+ Turn off your cell phone during sales calls and meetings.

+ It is usually proper to stand up to shake hands or when being introduced to someone.

+ Initiate the hand shake, connect comfortably and firmly. Look the other person in the eye. A couple of up and down shakes should do nicely. Avoid dead fish and King Kong hand shakes.

+ No smoking in or on customers premises. If you smell like cigarette smoke a lot of people consider it a lack discipline that you haven't quit. If you smoke you also "stink".

+ Gum chewing is a disconcerting activity unless you are a teenager, on the other hand chewing bubble gum while driving to stay awake is a good idea.

+ When visiting customer or prospect, please sit where you are told.

+ Keep pen and paper ready.

+ Keep small talk to a minimum.

5
Five Stories that Inspire

A MAN FOR ALL TIME

A few years before his death Winston Churchill was asked to deliver a commencement address at a widely known university in the UK. Known to ramble a bit they asked him politely to keep it short. After the introduction he rose slowly from his seat, grasped the podium firmly with both hands and looked at the audience intently. Turning his head to the left he said "NEVER GIVE UP" then turning to the right he said "NEVER GIVE UP", then to the center he repeated "NEVER GIVE UP". With that he nodded his head, smiled and returned to his seat. If you were there would you ever forget? He was the supreme salesman.

KNOCK – KNOCK, WHO'S THERE

You might recognize his name from the real-estate business. I have forgotten it, but I remember the story about him, it goes this way. Jim joined his father's real-estate firm at a young age. His father anointed him with the words that he needed to get listings of people who wanted to sell their home. If you get the listing you get a piece of the commission. Jim had the notion that if he walked the neighborhoods and knocked on doors and asked the owner if they wanted to sell their house he could get "listings". After the first week he had one listing. By the end of the first month he had three. He realized that the "Shoe Leather" was working. At each house he left his card and asked the home owner to call him when they wanted to sell their home. He was a nice guy and smiled a lot. He didn't give up. He found out his system worked. Perhaps you have already found that persistence works, cold calling is very hard on the body and self image, sometimes it's the only way. The early lessons taught him well.

EAT THE CAKE AND GET THE ORDER

This is a great true story. Ben was employed as a salesman for a big bakery. Cakes were their business. Ben did well, but a certain buyer at a large supermarket chain was always "too busy" to see him, so Ben started to leave a nice cake for him every Friday. He just dropped it off in the company box with his card. Time passed and one Friday Ben didn't leave a cake. On Monday morning Ben got a call from the super market buyer. He said "Where's my cake?" Ben said, "so sorry I forgot, but I will personally bring it over right now." Ben got in the door and had a new customer. The source for this story was of course Ben. We did photography work for Ben's company.

A CRAZY IDEA

Way back in 1958 over burgers and good coffee, at the local diner, Tony Ross a salesman friend was telling me a story. It occurred when he was a consultant to the Railway Express Company. This is how his crazy idea helped them solved a major problem.

The following is a little history you should know that goes with this story…before most of you were born, before super highways and massive trucking companies and before UPS and Fed Ex most all goods in this country were moved by the railroads or ships. All the major cities in this country are a result of being on a major railroad line or a major port. Back at this time there was a company called Railway Express. They were the UPS yesteryear. In the late 1940's they began to have a problem with breakage and damage of goods being shipped via their company. It was caused by careless handling by workers of Railway Express. It was costing the company big bucks in claims and they needed a way to bring this to the attention of the managers in all of the many local offices in the network. This is what Tony did…he shipped a corrugated box addressed to each manager labeled "A special gift for you".

Upon opening the box each found an attractive ceramic ashtray bro-

been displayed on their desk, useless. Annoyed and disappointed they complained to headquarters. Before shipping each ashtray it was broken with an intentional smack of a hammer! Complaints were ignored. A week or so later an unbroken intact ashtray was shipped. Upon opening they not only found an attractive one piece ashtray, but a note. It read something like this:

"Imagine how unhappy and disappointed you felt when the first ashtray arrived broken in pieces. Your feelings of anger and disappointment are just the way our customers feel when they receive a shipment damaged or broken by us at Railway Express. Please do your part to reduce customer complaints and claims. Our reputation is at stake. Thank you."

This is an almost explosive way to get your message across. The company was able to send its message in a non-offensive way without created an emotional response. This idea assisted greatly in correcting and minimizing the problem.

A TRUE STORY - THE DAY I GOT A SECOND CHANCE

Monday, December 13, 1971 dawned clear and sunny. I engaged Ron Hild Air Charters to fly me to Baltimore in his Piper Apache twin engine aircraft for a quick meeting with a client in the furniture business. Our meeting was successful and we agreed on the price to do the photography and catalog job. When we returned to Fairfield, Ron reminded me that we were all set for our Thursday charter to Lancaster, PA. The sole purpose of that trip was to make a presentation to Hamilton Watch Co. for their up-coming catalog. Four of us from the company would join Ron and his copilot, filling all six seats in the plane.

Our flight to Lancaster was made under overcast skies, but we had plenty of ceiling. The Apache landed uneventfully and we were on time for our meeting. On the way back to the airport it started to rain a little, but we were not concerned because we were pleased with the results of the meeting and our new client.

The plane was on automatic pilot and was headed to the airport in

Ron switched off the autopilot and took the plane down to 500 feet, hoping to spot the landing strip through the haze. I was beginning to wake up from my cat-nap when I heard Barry the copilot holler, "TREES DEAD AHEAD"! Ron attempted to gun the engines and climb, but it was too late. The propellers mowed the treetops. This immediately disabled the plane. Ron reached forward and turned off both engines. The ship was crippled, and we were going down. Ron yelled, "DOUBLE OVER".

The glass from the windshield started breaking up and flying back through the cabin as we smashed between the trees on a wooded hill-side. We tried to protect our eyes with our arms, but other pieces of the plane started mixing with the glass as small objects drummed into us. We came to rest in a wooded area near a residential neighborhood. The cabin incredibly missed all the large trees. My only thought was "God save us". The wings and engines were sheared off. The nose section, including the instrument panel, was peeled away and lay a few feet away from the gaping hole that was the front of the aircraft.

All was eerie and still as we lay there in the fog among the trees. I think we were all afraid to speak, but miraculously we were all alive. An employee of the local electric company was reading meters in the area and heard the crash. He was a Vietnam Veteran and knew the sound of a plane in trouble. He found us first and went for help. The North Haledon firemen rescued us and carried us down the steep hill to waiting ambulances, the art director survived with only a scratch and was able to walk away. The copilot Barry was the most seriously injured and spent five month recovering. The rest of us had injuries but not life threatening. I had surgery for a fractured vertebrae and that kept me in the hospital for ten weeks.

Two things come to mind as I reflect on that day many years ago. First thing I recall vividly was something incredible, as the plane was in its last agony of decent, a voice came to me clearly in that moment and said "Don, you are not going to die today". It was only later when my mind cleared that I understood that God had spoken to me. He had given me and all of us a second chance. God smiled on us that day.

The next day my mother and father came to see me in the hospital.

leaned over and looked hard into my face to make sure I was breathing. Next she raised her index finger into my face and said as only a mother can "I hope to God you have learned your lesson and slow down. The next time you might kill yourself." Then she kissed me on the forehead and cried. I realized I had better take stock…and I did. It was a wake-up call. I will admit that I did throttle back a little and I have flown only commercial airlines since.

6
Information & Sources to find Prospects and a Mailing List

You have probably found out that the computer is the most powerful source for finding information that has ever been invented. If you go to widely known search engines such as Google and type in anything to do with selling, marketing or advertising or more you will find a lot of organizations ready to sign you up and help you locate what you need. A lot of them are in business to sell you niche information. They will help you identify prospects in areas of manufacturing, services or communications and more. Before you decide to work with these people you need to explore the broader picture of information available from the U.S. Government as a beginning source before we go any further you hopefully know about the U.S. Governments Standard Industrial Classifications, better known as SIC numbers. Every company in the U.S. is listed and has a code number. The first part of the numerical system indicates the specific industry, the second part of the code spells out what part of that industry it belongs. You can get a free download of listing if you Google Manufacturing Directories or U.S.Gov. Manufacturers. In depth directories that go into detail about companies can be purchased from: Manufacturer's News, Inc. 1633 Central Street, Evanston, IL 60201, they publish books for each state in the union. Contains:

+ Full Company Name

+ Address

+ Phone

+ Names of decision makers

+ Yearly sales in dollars

+ Type of product or service rendered and are updated each year

This company has other very helpful services worth exploring. Go to Google: <u>mnistore.com</u>.

Another company for helping you target prospects and mailing list is Dun and Bradstreet. Known as D&B. They have programs that are specifically designed for small business. If you log on to <u>Zapdata.com</u> you can investigate some of their service. Their services are extensive and if you need in-depth reports of single or groups of companies D&B works.

Here is an example of how we use D&B to help with our mailing list.

1. We identified the industry SIC No's that matched the kind of companies we thought could use our services.

2. We listed the minimum gross sales we would accept as an indication of size. Companies that did less than five million a year in gross sales were excluded.

3. We used the telephone company's three digit area codes to designate the geographic regions. Using this manner of selection it was possible to fine tune areas that were not fruitful.

4. By using the system in #3 we could target cities in places where we didn't want to canvas the whole state. For example, not wanting all of Massachusetts we selected the area codes for Boston only etc.

5. Every three years we went through the same process. Eliminated areas that did not yield leads or sales and adding areas we hoped would perform better. Then we took the old and new lists and did a merge and purge in the computer. The final result was a "clean" and fresh mailing list. D&B's Marketing Services performed these functions and supplied us with a new list on a CD.

7
Be Prepared - Be a Boy or Girl Scout

Indicators that tell you if you are coming or going.

1. If you can't get your prospects interest or focus or eye contact pack up and leave.

2. If your prospect is accepting phone calls during your appointed time, you might try to reschedule, unless you just flew in from Boston. Patience is a virtue.

3. If you're *hoped for* customer doesn't have money, can't afford your product, and there is a low priced car in the "Reserved" parking space, it is time to hit the road.

4. If your prospect doesn't ask questions and is bored, your pitch is probably very uninteresting or the prospect has a helluva hangover. Try again another day. Check your presentation.

5. If you aren't getting anywhere with what appears to be an interested prospect, you are probably not asking for the order. You have become a professional visitor.

6. Finally be sure the person you are talking with makes the buying decisions. Talk to the Organ Grinder...Not His Monkey

8
Potholes on the Road to Success

As sales people we must recognize that we will make mistakes. Most are small errors in judgment and go unnoticed, but once in a while we mess-up big time. The bad ones are between you and your customer. When this happens it is not a good time to take a guilt trip or to rationalize with self justification. The good thing is that most of our stupidity can be fixed. As an example let us say you did not get "The Order" because you miscalculated the situation. Sometimes your client will let you requote if he has not given the project to your competition. What you do is ask your client if he would be kind enough to let you "Take a second look" and resubmit. This has worked for me on numerous occasions.

One time I missed an important appointment with a client and caught hell from her. I called a florist and sent flowers immediately with my profound apologies. When an order goes wrong or a misunderstand arises you must say you are sorry and fix it fast. If you let it go uncorrected you mess-up your reputation and usually will not hear from that customer again.

If things don't work for your in a certain job, change jobs. If you can't sell Cookies and Cake to a supermarket buyer you may well find out that you can be successful selling advertising commercials for a TV station. Never give up.

Here is a little story about my lack of immunity from stupidity.

We did quite a bit of business with clock companies and I finally got an appointment with the new sales manager at Seth Thomas in Connecticut. It took a couple of hours to get there. I had a new salesman with me I was going to show him how it was done. During the pre-

of Seth Thomas entered the conference room, we were introduced and shook hands. He smiled and asked in a strong voice "how much do you charge?" I responded smiling and said jokingly about as much as we can. His response was "this is the end of meeting". He left.

Lesson: You don't joke with the CEO.

9
Hey!
Have You Got a Minute?
Here Are Some Ideas to get Appointments
You Can't Sell Without Them

Presuming you have done your homework, you will need an information sheet with reference to the company and person you are going to telephone to make that appointment. You also need a script. Rehearse what you want to say so it sounds natural. Execs answer the phone with their name. Respond with your name and company, then say with a smile in your voice…." Have you got a minute"? Most of the time the answer will be YES, if the answer is NO, just ask when would be a better time to call. With a YES response tell the person you want a moment of time to show or explain how your company could improve what ever product or service offered. End your pitch with a request of "Would Wednesday morning be a good time to "Drop by"? (If not when) and finally if you have that appointment say "Thank you" and hang up. Now it is up to you.

The day of the week and the time of day you make appointment phone calls can make a difference in results. Typically, Monday's at the start of a business day, the telephone operator is busier than usual. It's not a good time to ask questions. Personally I found the best time for these calls is Wednesday and Thursday from 10AM to 3 PM. Frequently if you call before the phone operator arrives for work you will get to speak to some friendly person in the office who will be glad to pass you on to the person you are trying to reach. It is a little sneaky but it works.

Lets say you don't have the name of the person you need to speak with. Here is a suggestion or "little white lie" that has worked for me many times. When you reach the operator tell that person you want to send your corporate literature to the advertising, marketing, purchasing department or whatever and would like to have that person's name. It is unlikely you will be refused because this is a totally unthreatening request. Now that you have a name and title call back next week, hopefully the operator will not recognize your voice and will connect you. If you get that person's voice mail hang up and try again another time. Do not leave voice mail in an attempt to get an appointment.

Most businesses have cycles. As an example, Christmas trees, Matzo, American flags, flu shots. You get the picture. This has a lot to do with making the sale. If you are in the fertilizer business you know who and when you have to get the order for Spring delivery. In the toy business the new stuff is shown and sold in January and February and delivered in August and September. If you produce catalogs, you want to talk to the sales and marketing people at the toy company in November. Timing has everything to do with getting the business. The same goes for Jewelry trades who have their big showing of new "lines" in July, so you talk seriously to them in February.

10
Goal Setting

Personal goals are something every sales person should have. This is where you resolve to attain a better result based on your own performance. You desire to make more money so you expand the number of calls you make and cut your lunch hour. You might do some serious planning after hours at home. You may want to become a sales manager so you go to night school and study marketing. Reaching one goal begets another What gets you motivated? You may be a member of a sales force or you may be working on your own. As an individual, you can do more or do only what little you can get away with. You want to quit smoking or loose weight, reaching the goal is always up to you. Not reaching sales goals can result in not having a job.

A word for the boss man, President or Owner. Don't expect your sales people to reach objectives without giving them the tools. It is called Sales Ammunition such as: new products, advanced technology, expanded services or a mailing campaign to generate leads. Dazzling new literature will always gladden the heart of sales people. You need suggestions to help your sales people reach objectives. Discuss ideas at sales meetings and ask for ideas and discuss customer comments. Goal setting is important; it is a process. Don't be afraid to change course along the way to adjust and improve performance. Sales people work better if you give them a reason and incentives to reach targeted objectives.

11
Watch Out Where You Drop Your Pretty Shiny Marbles

This is a story about "Don't Drop Your Marbles in the Prospects Office." It is a parable about how unsmart you can be. Jack was very self assured. He almost strutted. Hair combed real neat, nice suit and tie. A good speaker. He was an account executive for an advertising agency. His name is Jack, short for Jack-ass. He had a very great idea, actually many great ideas about how he could improve sales at the ABC Company. He was hoping to get the advertising account. He presented a typed three page proposal of these sterling ideas to Sam Smart the Marketing Manager who listened intently as Jack did most of the talking at the meeting.

Sam was exceedingly impressed and even walked Jack out to the lobby and shook his hand warmly as he was departing. Sam Smart was happy to have the three page pitch Jack had left with him. Sam studied the proposals carefully for several days. He wrote a new proposal and went to see Mr. Excellent Boss in his pristine office. Sam presented his new marketing plan and Mr. Boss who was impressed with these sterling ideas (of stolen strategies) that he patted Sam Smart on the back for his great work.

In the meantime every time Jack called Mr. Smart, now VP of ABC, he was too busy or "out of town" to take the calls. Of course Jack realized his error when he noticed the new Ad campaign by ABC Co. The moral of this story don't leave all your neat ideas in the prospects office. Hopefully Jack realized he was a Jack-Ass. Don't give away the whole book, just the table of contents.

12

In Chaos Stay Organized

The only way to stay organized when you are juggling a lot of things at one time is to be a list person. Before we had laptops I kept my "To-Do" list on a lined yellow pad and attempted to update it every day in spite of interruptions. Laptops have made it easier and they work well anywhere. You wouldn't be caught dead without a cell phone or an iPod, would you?

All the unique compact portable devices available today make record keeping easy, fast, convenient and keep you organized. Written records are extremely important. Friday afternoon was my catch-up time to review and stay alert to the moment. If you are too busy to do this, you need to delegate or take stock of your work habits. What things are going on in your life that prevent you from keeping up? This introspection may require a close look at your work ethic. In the meantime slow down. Perhaps it is not so complicated to figure out what is blocking your way to a smoother procession of your work.

Do "First things First" and don't put off important or unpleasant issues until another time, bite the bullet, get it done, this way you remove the road blocks that stall your forward movement. Procrastination is a bad habit. If you "Face the Music" you will be able to play the tune better. Everyone who works under pressure needs a system that makes your business days satisfying and an agreeable event.

13
Five More Stories that Inspire

WHEN YOU ARE THE BUYER AND NOT THE PEDDLER

This is a story of how not to behave to a sales person regardless of what he or she is selling, particularly if he she is from IBM. Our receptionist gave me a business card from an IBM salesman who wanted to talk to the owner and that was me. I was curious what a salesperson from IBM would want with a photography studio cum catalog production house. I invited him to my office where we did the introduction stuff and he took a seat.

His opening words were "Do you do any word processing?" I replied with "what is word processing?" As I sit at my computer writing this story today it is the year 2009 and I have been word processing for ten years, but in 1984 I hadn't the remotest idea what he was asking. Mr. IBM continued speaking in terms I didn't understand. He told me it was the coming thing, my IBM electric typewriters would be replaced by computers and everybody was getting on board this technology surge and I better get with it or you'll be left in the dust. I got real uppity because of my ignorance and became defensive and even a little rude. I didn't care one rat's behind about this thing he was talking about and he finally saw he was not going anywhere, besides he could see he was wasting his time on an ignoramus who had not the insight or understanding. He stood and shook my hand in a gentlemanly manner and departed shaking his head slowly from side to side. My big mistake was not asking for some applications on how our company would and could use and benefit from his product etc, etc. I missed the boat and a good opportunity to learn what was thrust upon me years later. I was the jerk.

ALMOST A PURPLE HEART

The names of the participants have been changed to protect me from a law suit.

It was a cloudy Monday afternoon in February. Harry and Max were long time partners in their late fifties and were in the jewelry business. Harry ran the factory and Max took care of the sales. They sat in an office where their desks faced each other but were separated by a few feet to allow for a visitor chair, which was exactly where I was sitting at this instance. Max and Harry were having a serious disagreement about the content of pages ten and eleven of the catalog my company was preparing. I sat tensely in-between the partners, my head turning as in a tennis tournament. (Time out to explain something. The jewelry in question was in flat trays about eight by sixteen inches. The items were earrings in neat pairs in trays. Each partner had eight or nine trays spread out on his desk.) As their tempers increased, Max, using naughty words, stood up and started hurling jewelry trays at Harry. I hit the floor under Maxes desk. Harry returned the attack. Moments later it became quiet and I heard laughter. Max said as he was laughing "O.K. Don you can come out." Both partners were laughing. I emerged and sat. The office was a mess. One tray was stuck in a door near Harry's head. The partners made apologies all around, still laughing. I had to assume these spats occurred periodically. The meeting was over, but I returned the next day. All was well.

End note: The partnership lasted many years until they sold out and retired. The lesson I learned was never sit between two partners having a discussion.

IF THE SHOE FITS WEAR IT

I had three appointments in Pittsburgh. The early flight got me into the airport at 9 AM.

I was on my way in a Hertz by 9:30. The first two calls were a real bust and by 2 o'clock I said the hell with it and headed for the airport, but I saw a familiar street name that was a turn off for where I wanted to go for my last appointment. I took it and promptly got lost.

I was hot and tired but I saw a pay phone next to a deli and I made a call to the prospect because I really did have a 2:30 appointment with him. He said "You are only two blocks away you can't miss us." He was the owner of the Iron Age Safety Shoe Co. (a giant in the industry). Of all things he met me at the door and graciously guided me to his office. We exchanged greetings and I was smiling because he made me feel so comfortable. He showed me his existing catalog and said "tell me what is wrong with it?" I told him, the book was entirely without interest. The shoes were lined up like soldiers and had been photographed with the camera too close to the shoes and were big by the toe and skinny at the back which made them look like clown's shoes. So I said the shoes have the "Flatfoot floogie effect" I then explained and asked him if he would loan me a pair of shoes to take a test photo to prove my point.

Back in the Studio we did an uncomplicated photo and then juiced it with some props such as bricks and a masons trowel to create a work-ers environment. I flew back with the test picture the next week. After close inspection he said you have to meet our sales manager because you will be working with him on our new catalog. We went the extra mile and happily did their catalogs for many years thereafter.

BEING ALERT TO THINGS AROUND YOU

Prospecting is interesting. I knew a salesman who kept a pad and pen-cil on the seat next to him in his car. When he saw a truck with a busi-ness name that might be a lead, he would write it down…everything including the telephone number. He would do the same if he saw an interesting industrial building he'd record the name and town so when he got back to his office he'd check them out with a phone call or on the computer. A little hand held recorder is helpful.

14
The 50% Factor

My Father gave me some good advice many years ago. Son, he said "Believe about 50% of what you see, read and hear". Everyday in our lives we are subjected to exaggeration of the value of products, medical miracles, politictians and the advice of friends and the news media.

I am a devout skeptic.

Here are some things I am suspect about:

+ This may only be a rumor but joint arthroscopic surgery only works on 50% of subjects.

+ Many sophisticated pharmaceutical medicines only work on half the people they are supposed to help. Ask your doctor.

+ Bottled water is the biggest scam the public has ever fallen for.

+ If you eat organic food, are you feeling better?

+ And do you know what organic is?

This is how I found out about organic's. When in Japan after WW2, I was part of the occupation troops, at that time we were told not to eat any vegetables other than those fed us in the mess hall. Those Japanese veggies were real organic, they even looked good, however they used human waste to fertilize vegetable gardens. We take a lot of chances with people who say "Trust Me". Be a little skeptical about all the claims you hear, in particular from people who want to help you invest your money or buy their products. Challenge them. Read the fine print. If people call you a cynic show them your burn marks and scars. One last thought: When you are offered a job and you are told you can make more money in the selling game than you ever dreamed of and you won't have to work very hard to do it, take a walk. There is no excellence without labor, unless you are a liar, con artist or plain dishonest. Remember the old addage: Fool me once, shame on you – fool me twice – shame on me. Cynics win, trust me. . . it's just common sense.

15
Where's the Magic?

In times of yore, the only so called magic words that got my attention were: Free and New, until I found out that nothing was Free and New was not. If you are writing sales letters or even copy for TV or print media you will soon learn that there are no magic words. You may disagree and say that there are three magic words that always work, such as "I love you", the concept is undoubtedly pleasing when spoken by an ardent suitor, but beware that the repetition of those words will be required throughout life to maintain a meaningful relationship with the loved one. Having said this, let us return to the use of words we use in business. Semantics is the study of the meanings of words. As you know you can use different words to convey the same meaning but good selection can put a stronger or milder inference to what you write or say. Your computer can be a tremendous help. Right click on a word and the list synonyms pops-up. For example try *"Pain"*, ache, hurt, soreness, sting, tenderness, twinge, throb, all depict same thing but in different degrees of intensity. The real magic of words is how you arrange them in order to express yourself in exactly the way you want the reader to understand in a meaningful way. Where does the charm of words come from? It comes from you the speaker, the writer because when you choose the right words and say them enthusiastically, with conviction and use a friendly, smiling voice, people are influenced and will be more apt to believe what you are saying. If you have a limited vocabulary you will experience difficulty in the your ability to express yourself. Reading books is one way to increase your vocabulary. Good communicators and successful sales people have a way with words. Do this and you will reap the rewards.

16
Three Men, Each a Cornerstone

B efore you were born there existed three men who wrote books that had the selling game all figured out.

Dale Carnegie, <u>How to Win Friends & Influence People</u>

Frank Bettger, <u>How I raised myself from Failure to Success in Selling</u>

Elmer Wheeler, <u>How to Sell Yourself to Others</u>

(These books are available through the internet, libraries and some book stores.)

Each of these men wrote many more books but the ones listed should be read first.

In my opinion these gentlemen were the basis of modern selling fundamentals. They are the foundation on which many of today's author's stand. They understood the tremendous value of personality training not only in selling but daily life. We all know that the pearls of wisdom said by these men are as true today as they were in the past. In our hearts we know that we don't use these wise practices enough in our daily work. This would be a good reason to obtain these books and keep handy for reading at home or waiting to see a prospect.

17
Websites are Good but No Big Deal

Today, big and small companies have websites. They are quite useful to describe products and avenues by which customers can obtain the products and information. A website increases your exposure and as you know, serves an important purpose. If your company has a website, be sure to give prospects your web address. In addition your website must be maintained on a frequent basis or it will get stale. If your company advertises in trade journals be sure to invite the reader to log on to your website. Don't bury the web address in small type at the bottom of the ad. You have probably figured out that a website is not the ultimate, however it is a helpful tool, but not the end-all. It is a billboard at the side of the road.

18
Advertising is like Oxygen,
You Can't Survive Without it

In selling, you tell them what you are going to tell them, then you tell them, then you tell them what you told them.

Consistency in advertising is best defined as repition of your sales message at unbroken intervals. It is absolutely imperative for the growth of a business and its continued exsistance.

Early on I received this counsel from an old-time salesman who told me that if you use direct mail you must mail consistently to get results. We followed this advice and did all sorts of mailing campaigns; Mailings were sent six or more times a year. The mailings that got the best results were what we called "Sampler Mailings". As said earlier, we produced catalogs for manufacturers and importers. When a customer agreed we would print more of his catalogs than he needed and use the overruns as part of our mailing campaign. Since our printer would also benefit from the promotional mailing, he charged us only for the paper, the press time was on the house. A letter and reply card were enclosed with the sample catalog. The response came by phone or the reply cards. The return on investment paid off. It gave us good, solid leads and in the long run was responsible for our growth.

19
Assorted Stuff to Keep in Mind

Follow your intuition and listen to that little voice within. Don't listen to people who hang the crepe and tell you it can't be done or who say "Now is not a good time", they don't know your business. Moses didn't listen and neither did Thomas Edison.

+ Don't let enthusiasm overshadow your good judgment. What's hot today is in the scrap heap next week.

+ Read to gain knowledge.

+ Learn something technical.

+ Step out of the box to be creative.

+ Try new things - Experiment!

+ Think twice before hiring relatives and friends. This is where agreements in writing aren't worth the paper they're written on. Hurt feelings last & last.

+ Profit Is Not a Dirty Word.

+ Partnerships are either successful or a disaster rarely in-between.

+ Everyday, tell your wife you lover her. Hug your kids and pet the dog.

+ Universal truths are usually not.

+ If you prophesize the dark side of things, watch out they do not become "Self fulfilling" .

+ Selling really is an enjoyable profession. Have fun and play by the rules.

20
How Many of These Things Can You Do?

- ☐ Your own laundry
- ☐ Polish your shoes
- ☐ Sew on a button
- ☐ Change a diaper
- ☐ Shoot baskets
- ☐ Fix a toy
- ☐ Make a bed
- ☐ Open the door for a lady
- ☐ Change a tire
- ☐ Plant a flower
- ☐ Husk corn
- ☐ Make a fire in the fireplace
- ☐ Row a boat
- ☐ Sit by a lake
- ☐ Watch a sunset with a friend
- ☐ Turn off the TV
- ☐ Go fishing with a kid
- ☐ Hold a hand
- ☐ Open a can
- ☐ Fry an egg
- ☐ Hold a kitten
- ☐ Smile when you can't
- ☐ Give gifts
- ☐ Accept gifts gratefully
- ☐ Give of yourself
- ☐ B.... li.. wh.. y.. c..'.

☐ Kiss ass when you must
☐ Accept apologies
☐ Never argue with a police officer
☐ Say hello to strangers
☐ Learn to read upside-down
☐ Send birthday cards
☐ Honor our Flag
☐ Save money
☐ Give money
☐ Thank God
☐ Pray

WHAT'S YOUR SCORE?

21
Morality 101

Common sense is not common. We call it common sense because
it is universal to our actions and reactions. Our morality decides
the choices we make, it influence who we become. Our conscience, our
beliefs of right and wrong become our personal set of guidelines. If you
were in Scouting in your youth you might remember you had to be
twelve years old to join and part of the test was to recite the Scout Law:

A SCOUT IS:

*TRUSTWORTHY, LOYAL, HELPFUL, FRIENDLY,
COURTEOUS, KIND, OBEDIENT, CHEERFUL,
THRIFTY, BRAVE, CLEAN AND REVERENT.*

For a twelve year old that is asking a lot. How about those of us well
beyond that age. Wow, what a list of rules to live by, but that more or
less sums it up. Which ones have we forgotten? As for myself I would
confess to not being 100%. It is easy to step around things that are
unpleasant and we all do it. The bottom line is to be consistent about
those things that truly matter. If you have a worthy destination "Stay
the Course".

22
Farming for Sales

You might consider farming an odd way to talk about selling, but there are many similarities. First of all the soil needs to be rich in nutrients to yield a good crop. You on the other hand need good territory to cultivate plentiful sales. Secondly the farmer wants a sturdy barn, the proper tools and a tractor. You need a company that is vigorous and strong that will support you with the right marketing information, equipment and a comfortable car to get to the grazing land. The farmer will fertilize his fields, he will select and plant the seed that produce the best price at market and hopefully will have a good harvest. You will be planting seeds where ever you go. However, all your seed will not germinate during the first season or perhaps the second. As a matter of fact, not all the seed you plant will actually germinate into sales. However, if you sow enough seed your harvest will be bountiful. To make this happen it will be necessary to eliminate weeds, spread some fertilizer, and water the soil to prevent drought.

The moral of this story is: Don't go barefoot in a cow pasture on a hot day, unless you wear boots.

23
Go to Trade Shows for Big Returns

Trade shows can be a great place to find prospects and to discover changes that are happening in your field of business. Every February in New York City the Toy Fair trade show happens. Manufacturers and importers gather in their show-rooms at 200 5th Ave and invite buyers from all over the country to see the newest and hottest selling items. You must register at the door to gain admittance. Trade shows do not admit the public or anyone not related to that line of business. They want to talk to customers. The buyers who attend must show their business card identifying themselves as legitimate to receive an entry badge. If you are not a potential buyer you can't get in! I found this out when I naively presented my business card and was told to get lost. I returned to my office and had my art director design a business card that used a fictitious store name, my title was Buyer. It was fancied-up and we printed it out, trimmed to size and saved some for next year. I returned the next day with my phony business card. It got me a badge into the show. When you get into a trade show it pays to be careful how you conduct yourself. You never approach a busy booth or showroom. Walk the whole show first and pick the cherries i.e. the subject that looks the most promising as a potential client. Trade shows can last up to a week, most are three days. It may take several days to accomplish your survey and make contacts. I never tried to sell anything to anyone at a show. If the booth or showroom was quiet I could walk in and look around, I would always be approached by a sales person and that gave me the opportunity to explain my services and of course get names. Later, in a week or so I started to make phone calls and make appointments.

About that fake business card, I never felt it was deceitful, after all I was selling something they truly needed. And I was doing my job. Oc-

me a pass. There are more ways than one to gain admission. You could carry an envelope and tell the gatekeeper you needed to make a delivery.

How do you learn about trade shows? Here is a good way, when you call on a prospect or a customer and you are waiting in the lobby you will usually find "Trade" magazines piled up on an end table. Take one with a subscription card and slip it into your case. Subscribe. You will soon get free trade journals in your mail. If you find yourself taking part in a trade show be sure to walk around, find your competitors and make friends, network with them, it really is a small world. Keep walking you never know what you will find. Collect and hand out your business cards. Collect catalogs and brochures from your competitors and related companies. Large companies will sometimes give big cocktail parties and invite customers and attendees of the show. These social gatherings are held after hours in a showroom or a nearby hotel. Invitations are verbal. Normally you can walk right in. I traveled to trade shows in Boston, New York, Atlanta, Chicago and Vegas and places I have forgotten.

Last bit of information: Trade shows are held for every major or minor industry in the world, Google for info – wear comfortable shoes and drink some Red Bull.

24
Be Safe

This is something I tell all my grandchildren "Be Safe" Would you know what I meant if I said it to you? Here is what I mean when I say it to Tyler who is at college in Boston. Don't go nutty with the booze and parties, don't do intimate things with girls unless you protect them and yourself. Choose your friends carefully. College is not holiday time it is the last chance to learn stuff you will need for the rest of your life. It simmers down too: MODERATION IN ALL THINGS. If you follow this dogma life will be easier to manage through many problems. Here are a few things to consider: Use credit cards only in emergency. If you borrow money make sure you have a program to pay it back in a reasonable time. As you know credit card companies will eat you alive. Go back and read the Boy Scout Law. It says it all. If you think this stuff is BS, remember life has a peculiar way of pay-back. Other thing that belong on this list; don't drive while intoxicated with any substance. Guns Kill. Don't play the other guys game, you'll loose. Stay out of bad places. I'll stop the list here, you don't really need a list Be careful, BE SAFE.

25
Ancient Proverbs from the Old Guy on the Mountain

- When you sell Look Rich, when you buying Look Poor.
- Always build the outhouse downhill from the kitchen.
- Drink upstream, pea downstream.
- Don't lie-down with dogs; you will get-up with fleas.
- Don't cast your pearls before swine.
- Joy is free, euphoria is drugs and neither lasts.
- Old Age is not golden, it is rust.
- If you live an absolutely pure life, you will have no fun.
- Carry a big stick, but not around children.
- Anger will soften if you wait until tomorrow.
- Forgiveness is the greatest gift.
- Know the difference between passion and love.
- Money in the bank is a soft pillow at night.
- Thieves can be the nicest people.
- Keep a level head and your feet on the ground.

26
A Few Tips on Remembering Names

All of us have a name. It is on our birth certificate. It is very important. It is with us all our life. Few people are willing to change it. It is truly the most important thing you own. When I heard about an evening class at a nearby college that might improve my memory I signed up. The most useful thing I learned was a system for remembering names. If I don't put that system into practice immediately when I meet someone I will undoubtedly forget their name.

This is the procedure. The subject is anyone you want to greet and get to know. At the appropriate moment you approach the person stick out your hand, smile and say hi or hello, my name is: your name, if the subject responds with nice to meet you and doesn't give you a name, ask for it. Subject responds Mario, you say (repeating his name) Mario, nice to meet you, (find some other thing to say so you can use his name again. Now it will stick until you can write it down. Repetition is the trick. You have said the name three times. It is called visualizing. This is how it works. Here are some names and how I visualize or picture something that will give me a hint, because you will find that all you need is a hint, just a small clue to recall a whole name.

Example: Mr. Fred Weber, picture in your minds eye a spider web, that hint should bring back to mind the whole name including his first name. The other day I met for the first time a couple with the last name of Weld. Her name was Jean and her husbands name was Jerry. This may sound "way out", but it works. I pictured two pieces of metal welded together, the welding seam going right down the middle of my mental picture. On the left side of the weld I put a piece of blue jean fabric and on the right side I placed a bold letter J. That is the entire hint I will forever remember their names.

I could never remember my daughter's cell phone number. I needed some sort of device that would hold it in my memory bank. Her number is 208-715-2307. This is what I did. The area code is easy to remember so I didn't do anything with it, the 715, I made into a time of day, The hands of the clock were at 7:15, the 2307 broke apart into 23 and 07. 23 was the number on a house I used to live in and 07 reminded me of agent 007. As long as you remember the memory clues you will remember. The cell phone number is done with a form of memory hooks, the other is repetition and visualization so it will remain in your memory. This is not a childish method, it works all the time. Practice and it becomes second nature. I have just scratched the surface of this subject. You may want to go a step further and locate a book called <u>Stop Forgetting</u> originally authored by Dr. Bruno Furst, edited and re-released and revised by Lotte Furst & Gerrit Storm a Doubleday publication.

27
The Title of This Book
and How I Found It:
Unseen, Untold Is Unsold

This is the story of how I found a slogan that seemed to fit the photography, catalog business and almost any business.

My insurance agent who was a friend called me late one Friday and asked for help on a small project. His father owned and operated an upholstery shop and was closing the business, in fact retiring. Would I come over Saturday morning and help clean out the place? Arriving amid a flurry of activity, I was assigned to remove all the clipping and fragments of paper notes from a very large bulletin board. I was told I didn't have to save the thumb tacks. His father wanted all those small pieces of paper he had accumulated over a twenty five year period, five deep on the bulletin board. I toiled away at my arduous job, reading the notes here and there – "Call Mrs. Shapiro her chair is ready". There was an ad for a used Packard car and another on a torn brown paper bag saying "order webbing" and many more. Who would want to save this stuff? When I neared the bottom of his layered mass, I found a gem. Perhaps it was torn out of a magazine or newspaper, it was what it said that caught my attention. Unseen, Untold is Unsold. It was a masterpiece of understatement. It fit my business to a T. The scrap of paper went into the box of mementos, but I did write the little nugget on the back of my business card. Not realizing it at the time but I had just saved a slogan which my business would be known for years to come. It was used on all our sales literature. One of our customers made us 500 beautiful wood plaques with the slogan that we gave to our customers and potential customers. A client in the Jewelry business even made us tie tacks and cuff links with the slogan.

It was catchy and true. In a weak moment I wrote a very bad poem about it...turn the page

28
Epitaph to a Peddler

His motto he extolled and is now a rule of gold
It reminds us of the power of these words so bold
Thru his years of toil and sincere good selling
His motto he developed and to all was telling
And now he is rich from what he sold
Because he lived by the words he told
On his deathbed, a day so cold
These last words he tried to say
His breath came short, his eyeballs rolled
But finally four words his lips did mold
UNSEEN, UNTOLD is UNSOLD
And on his tombstone they chiseled it deep
Everyone said they wanted it to keep

29
Bless This Day

When in the course of time you are favored by the Almighty and cross the threshold of a prospect who wants to buy your product, all you really need to do is smile, shake hands and sit down. Answer his questions, keep your mouth shut and let the buyer do the talking. He will know what he wants, he will know how many and he will know about your company. Answer questions, don't rush and write-up the order. This buyer is pre-sold. Don't distract him or her with your mouth. Don't talk yourself past the order. Recognize this situation and act accordingly. One of the best questions to ask is, if you don't already know, "When do you want delivery". Say "Thank You" several times. Situations such as this are rare, but when they happen it is like sipping cool spring water.

30
Two Aces are Not a Full House

This is what happens when you get too content with just several high return customers as an alternative to many.

There were four of us at this particular time selling and servicing accounts. Three of us had clients that kept things lucrative and busy, but Jack had just two. The dollar return on those two accounts almost equaled my yearly sales. One of Jacks customers was AT&T. The other client was a large supermarket chain who bought photography for their weekly flyers. He was happy and satisfied. One day Jack got some bad news. The supermarket account was taking their photography "In house". They bought a digital camera of their own and would no longer need his services. He lost 50% of his business overnight and his other account, AT&T was in Titanic mode at the time, but Jack didn't see the waves. Fortunately AT&T stayed afloat long enough for Jack to scramble and pick up new accounts.

This is an interesting exception. One of our customers in the lighting industry had so much business with Sears they put their best salesman in the Sears Chicago office full time to make sure everything went smoothly. This is called rear guard protection. It worked well for about three years, however the competition began to get so fierce with the lighting products coming from China that Sears had no choice but to change suppliers and buy from the Chinese. Guess who they hired as their buyer of lighting products? You guessed it. It was our watch dog at Sears from the U.S. Manufacturer. The U.S. company went out of business and we lost a good customer.

Economic circumstances can take you out of the win column into the loss column. You have little control. As a sales person, you need to listen to all the gossip and ascertain for yourself which direction the smoke is going. Surely you get the point. There is safety in numbers. Read the Wall Street Journal. You don't need to be a genius to figure things out for yourself. Trust your gut feeling; don't draw your enlightenment from the crowd at the tavern. Knowledge will warn you when to consider making strategic changes. Protect yourself; don't go down with the ship.

31
Go to the Head of the Class

As of this writing I am considered an old man. Perhaps not as wise as I would like to think, but certainly I have observed much and learned from that. Learning comes from observation and wisdom comes from understanding how we apply these positive or negative discoveries and skills. We see what kind of behavior works in our favor and the frivolity of other forms of action or the lack of it. This is fundamental. Here's the trick. Certain actions are unique and generic to what we are. A salesperson listens to another salesperson and learns that particular selling technique just as a surgeon learns a new skill at the operating table by observing another in action. Know when to turn on your attention receptors to absorb and store what you have seen and heard. Focus your concentrated attention during these moments. The message is: observe and listen selectively and remember. Always discard the BS, you will know it when you hear it.

32
Stress Is a Worldwide Condition

Stress is not depression. Like salt a little stress is good. When examining the subject of stress you must try to separate personal and business stress. You can't do much about home-style stress while on the job. Set it aside for the time being. Business stress is problems you face every day, many are unexpected. Most of the time stress is a condition that can not be attributed to any one factor but is a combination of many. Anger can be a symptom of stress, check your feelings and speak softly. Here are some ways people have found to ease the pain of stress: Exercise such as walking or going to the gym. Meditation works for some and prayer works for many.

Some people seem to have an unlimited ability to handle stress. Perhaps that is why they are administrators or even the boss. Most sales people I know handle daily stress quite well. One way is to ignore it and hope it goes away, surprisingly the causes of stress just disappear as new ones appear. Some people like stress. They clutch problems to their bosoms as if they were a badge of honor. They tell you how bad things are, commiserate a bit, give some words of understanding and don't stay too long. Did these last few words help you with your stresses? Probably not. Like death and taxes they never go away. You have to learn to live with them. Humorously the word stress rhymes with, mess, obsess, distress, endless and so forth. It is an integral part of our being, inescapable. The following are some words of wisdom from anonymous sources.

+ Life without chaos and pandemonium would be boring. Learn to enjoy martinis.

+ Believe that some days you are the pigeon and some days you are the statue.

+ Always keep your words soft and sweet just in case you have to eat them.

+ Drive carefully, it's not only cars that can be recalled by their maker.

+ If you put both feet in your mouth at the same time, you won't have a leg to stand on.

+ Be the second mouse, he gets the cheese.

+ Birthdays are good for you, the more you have the longer you live.

+ You may be only one person in the world, but you may be the world to one person.

We can learn a lot from crayons…some are sharp, some are pretty and some are dull. Some have weird names and all are different colors, but they all have to live in the same box.

33
The Black Box

Date October 1948. A guy walks into my store front photo studio holding a black box about the size of a small trunk. He said "Do you want to make some money?" How could I say no? I had only been in business since July, I said "Yeah". He set the box down and asked me if I knew how to make Photostats, I said, "No I don't." He said "You got a darkroom?" "Yes," I replied. "I'll show you how to make Photostats right now". In the darkroom he showed me how to make a Photostat in four minutes.

The black box was a simple contraption. It had light bulbs in the bottom of the box, a piece of milk white glass about ten inches above the bulbs and a lid with a piece of sponge rubber to hold two sheets of paper together on the glass when the lights in the box went on. When the exposure was complete and developed, you had a negative image of the document the customer wanted copied. Repeat the process using the negative and you had a positive image of the customer's document. The material cost fifty cents and you could charge $3.00 for the copy, less for more copies. In the mid to late 1950's the Xerox company began selling the Xerox duplicating machine and ultimately put us happily out of the stat business, it had served its purpose. This is a simple example of selling a cold drink to a very thirsty person.

In 1948 there were no office copiers, no fax machines or push button telephones. The whole point of this story is that in just a few words, I was ready to buy. This person who taught me how to make stats was smooth, friendly and he genuinely seemed to want to help me. I bought, he didn't sell. He knew the answers but let me ask the questions. He gave me a nice discrete sign to put in the window. I paid him on the spot $110 for the black box and two sizes of regular and legal photostat paper. He gave me his card and told me to call him when I wanted more stat paper.

This service brought in people from all over town. I met a lot of nice folks and generated new photography business. The black box paid the rent and more. This salesman showed me the need and how it would generate traffic and make new customers. It was products I could use and he taught me how to use it. Consider these things that will help your customers as you go about your business. They are called pro-points.

34
Helpful Habits for
a Successful Career

---

1. Get out of bed in the morning before the alarm goes off.

2. Take care of yourself both physically and mentally.

3. Share work at home and the office.

4. The biggest secret to a happy life is to live within your means and plan for the future.

5. Taking all the above into consideration remember that the unexpected happens.

35
The Elements of Salesmanship

Try these words, somehow they all seem to share.

- Friendship - making new.
- Scholarship - learning how.
- Courtship - finding the right one.
- Sportsmanship - fair play.
- Swordsmanship - parry or thrust.
- Relationship - what life is about.
- Partnership - trusting.
- Leadership speaks for itself.

36
Links to Survival When on the Road!

Is your vehicle equipped for the road? Do you have the simple things on board to keep you comfortable and safe. Let us start with easy stuff: gas tank full, tires in good shape, wipers that don't streak in the rain, heater and AC working and your cell phone. All this stuff is elementary. Here is what else you need and it won't break the bank: an empty soda bottle with drinking water, a couple of energy bars in the glove compartment, bubble gum to chew and keep you awake when your head nods, maybe a little hard candy for a spurt of energy near the end of the day, a blanket just in case, Triple A or equivalent.Many car insurance companies offer road service with your policy at no extra charge, get it, you never know.

37
Please Turn on the Light

Reflections on a life with and without a camera have led me down many paths. Fifty years in business, in particular the commercial photography business, has taught me countless lessons that have nothing to do with a camera or making photographs. They were the lessons of business. Had I gone to Harvard Business School, the road may have been smoother but as it turned out I attended RIT and then the school of hard knocks. There are certain mistakes you make in business that you never make again.

Furthermore if you are not a calculated risk taker or you hesitate when opportunities arise, then you will not progress and wonderful opportunities may pass you by.

You get better at evaluating opportunity the longer you are in business. You just get smarter and trust your own judgment because you have traveled the road. There is an old saying "He who hesitates is lost". It can best be illustrated when you are bidding at an auction and you hesitate at the last moment. You loose because you hesitated.

It is said that "Old age is no place for sissies", you don't have to be old to be a sissy. Being a sissy is a poor mental format for running a business or for that matter being a salesperson. Making YES decisions is just as important a knowing when to say NO.

38
May Real Friends Have Champagne and Sham Friends Have Real Pain

Friends are friends, customers are customers, clients are clients and finally business friends are business friends. There are rare exceptions when you click with someone in business and you have a real friend. This issue is delicate and I will admit it is my opinion but I can only recall having two real close friends with a business relationship that lasted through all sorts of twists and turns of life. I think going out to lunch and an occasional golf date are fun and surprisingly, you may find your customer thinks the same way. When you are the buyer and the sales person gets too friendly or chummy, it is difficult to terminate that relationship and replace this sales person with a new vendor when all you really want to do is change suppliers. This applies, To Whom It May Concern: Accountants, Insurance agents and your Lawyer. You are trapped by a heavy duty business friendship. As a salesperson, the inverse may also become a problem for you. There is nothing like a solid, trusting business, i.e. professional friendship. It is your job as a sales person to build trust and confidence. It is important you keep your clients satisfied and comfortable. Keep in mind that moderation in all things will center your life.

39
He Had All of Me in His Hands

I was in business for several months and was getting used to people walking into the studio to sell something or ask for a donation. I was not prepared for Lewis Kellsey. He was at least 78 years old. He was well-dressed, a tall slender man with gray hair. He wore rimless glasses and a fedora. He introduced himself as representing the Deardorf Camera Co. He wanted to know if I had one. I said no. Mr. Kellsey took the camera out of its case and unfolded it. It was made of mahogany, stainless steel parts and black leather bellows. It glowed. It was a view camera that had no peer. You could take pictures on 8x10in. film. The camera folded down to the size of a 4 inch stack of Time magazines. I knew immediately that I absolutely had to have this jewel. It was beautiful. Kelsey could see I was drooling. Kellsey said point blank "Mr. Hults if you don't have one of these cameras you are NOT in the commercial photography business". He took off his coat and sat down. This camera I knew about but never dreamed of buying one...yet. It could correct every form of distortion and could twist and turn like a hula dancer. Just like magic, Mr. Kellsey brought forth a small black box. It contained a sparkling new lens that fit the camera. He put it in my hand, it was a new Kodak Ektar, the best lens you could buy back in 1949. I had to have this camera and lens. Before I could ask Mr. Kellsey, he answered the big question...the price was, including the lens $2,450.00. I asked Mr. Kellsey if he would meet with me and my father for lunch the next day at the diner across the street to discuss the purchase.

I never saw anyone talk to my father like Mr. Kellsey. Before I could take a bite out of my hamburger my father was buying the camera, the lens, a carrying case, 8 film holders, a heavy duty tripod and a focusing cloth because Kellsey said I had to have this other stuff to use the camera. My dad loaned me the money and I paid him back in 14 months. In those days there wasn't a bank in the world that would loan a 23 year old kid photographer that kind of money. By the time we had been in business forty years, we had 32 Deardorf cameras on the floor of a 30,000 sq.ft. photography studio. Why did I tell you this story? When you offer a jack hammer to a guy using a crowbar you are sure to make a sale. When you know he cannot move forward in his business without the tools you supply you know you are at the right place at the right time.

40
Keep the "Close" Simple - Sometimes It's Only About Money

Once upon a time there was a salesman sitting with his customer hoping for a response that would indicate that he was ready to buy or as it is said, "sign on the dotted line". The customer stopped to take a breath and the sales person asked a simple question "Do I have the order". The response was a simple "yes, when can we have delivery." Does this sound too simple? Do you think you need a bunch of fancy trick questions to get a yes answer? Are you afraid to simply ask for the order. "I want your business Mr. Brown, what do we need to do today so we can begin to ship the product you need or when can we start to do the design work on your new building or when can I send my tailor to measure you for that new suit?"

Once when I was just starting out I was confronted with a wise old geezer for whom I wanted to do a big photo assignment. I asked one of those "close the sale" questions I read in a book thinking I was real slick, the gent smiled at me and simply said "Why don't you just ask for the order son". Something went click and I refrained from smart alec stuff ever again. If you keep searching for the magic words, you are wasting your time. Be honest, be frank, be friendly, smile and ask for the order.

There are some questions you can ask to get the discussion off dead center. They all have to do with money because that is the biggest little obstacle you must get by to close the sale. If there is a goodly sum of money involved, have you done credit checks in advance. Here are some questions you should ask when the customer wants you to reduce your price.

    1. If you will give me a deposit and pay us on delivery I will do
so&so

2. We can offer a 2% ten days, would that work for you?

3. If you give me the order today, we can make terms such as a small deposit now and the balance 30-60 days after delivery.

Don't give the store away, calculate what you might have to do before you arrive for the appointment. Balloon the price a little before-hand so you have room to maneuver. There are numerical considerations for payment. Ask the customer what he or she had in mind. If the prospect doesn't have the money for any of your suggestions, wish him well and move on.

What does all this have to do with salesmanship? It is all part of getting the business. If your prospect says his company can't afford your prices at this time, find out if there isn't an alternative, such as a 5 story building instead of 7 or a 16 paged catalog instead of 24. Be creative. Remember you are on his side, it's not a war. I haven't said anything about fancy schmancy closing techniques. Be a Gentleman.

41
Can We Talk? - It's Personal

Well, I had to talk about God sooner or later. If you don't want to listen just skip this part. I am steadfast in my faith but I don't stand on street corners handing out tracts or join in demonstrations. Most of us who embrace our relationship with God don't do nutty things or wear our beliefs on our shirt sleeve. We do try to do good things quietly and go to worship service regularly. I do know it would be very difficult to live life without God. He must love and care for me because He has saved my life twice and guided me through serious personal and business crises. Maybe you think you can handle all the tough stuff yourself, but why not get all the help you can. Talk to God, the line is never busy; It can be a lifesaver.

The Movie "The Tuskegee Airmen" is a true story and takes place during WW2. It has a scene where a fighter pilot is having a dialogue with his flight commander. This young airman is depressed and makes a comment that he doesn't think there is a God. His superior officer snaps back, "If you don't believe in God you had better have a damned good substitute". If God is only your copilot you better swap seats. Never be ashamed to ask God for help and never be reluctant to say thank you in your prayers. In the tough and competitive world of sales and the fox holes of life it is hard to be an atheist. A retired U.S. Marine told me that there are only two defining forces that have ever offered to die for you. One is Jesus Christ and the other is the American soldier. One died for your soul and the other died for your freedom.

The Holy Bible is my rule book. Try Proverbs in the Old Testament, it offers good advice.

42
Are You Winning the Big One?

You are not born with it, you can't live without it. The good news is that it is a skill you can acquire. You can keep as much as you want. You can loose it and still get it back. The more you keep, will make you more proficient in your career. The more you have, the better you'll be. It's SELF CONTROL.

Here are some opinions where your self control is vital.

+ If it is about money, it is the most difficult to control.

+ Increase your means or decrease your needs.

+ What makes you angry? Identify the triggers and write them down. Try visualizing a STOP sign when anger strikes. Remember those who make you angry control you. Anger is prehistoric, it is also a learned behavior. Test yourself, try to be cool the next time you drive your car in traffic.

+ The following can ruin your health. Smoking cigarettes is expensive and you either quit or sooner or later you will get sick. Booze in moderation works for most, alcoholism is a roller-coaster ride to hell. Drugs are the end, forget it.

+ Eat healthy doesn't mean fries and cheese burgers for lunch every day. The presumption is that your I.Q. is over 100, so you should know better. Fast food places still sell salads. Ask yourself "Who's winning, your body or you?"

+ A final word about self control. If you attempt to do it all at once, you will fail. Pick one thing and work on it, when you have success go to the next item on your list. Don't let the little annoyances get under your skin. There are no short cuts.

- It helps to bear in mind that your destination is a place you want to reach but it is usually the trip you remember the best.

43
Money Is Not the Root of All Evil

If you had a million dollars what would you do with it? Most ordinary folks would say they would pay their bills or any outstanding debts. Good start. What's next? Put enough aside to pay the taxes on that money – absolutely. Then find a safe place to put the rest of it. That is what I want to talk about now. Successful sales people will make "good" money and that is as it should be, but good sales people have one problem in common, they are very susceptible to the influence of other good sales people. To put it another way, success enjoys spending money. Does any of this sound familiar? When you have had a good day, week or month you want to reward yourself for a great performance, right? Don't deny it. However you have an obligation to yourself and family to put money aside for emergencies and special needs. If you are into "get rich quick" you will wonder where your money went. This leads me to a statement that is now key to a good nights sleep. KEEP THAT WHICH YOU SAVE – SAFE. There are thousands of people out there who want to help you. Listen, but you don't have to buy-in. You are not obligated to purchase just because these people give you a pitch. Don't be a sucker! Safety starts with a bank, and any money you put into a bank for Savings Accounts, CD's i.e. Certificates of Deposit and Money Market accounts are insured by the FDIC. You are insured as an individual for a max of $250,000. You and your spouse would be covered for $500,000. Using individual accounts. Your money is safe. No one can take it away from you. FDIC, The Federal Deposit Insurance Corporation is part of the Government of the USA if the Fed goes down then everything goes with it, that includes you and me, but this is not likely. It is obvious that the banks are the safest and a good place to start. It is true that banks do not pay a high rate of interest on your money, but if you want your money safe, then this is where you go.

Gamblers are not savers. Don't roll the dice and play poker or twenty one unless you are a card counter. There is one thing I have left out. Real Estate is usually an investment that pays off, you must be patient. In any financial obligations there will be paper to sign. Always read the fine print. If you don't understand, make the person who wants your signature explain it thoroughly so you do understand. Legal wording is not always easily understood, even by lawyers. Watch out for clauses that penalize you for early withdrawals. If you buy an Annuity, be careful there are many varieties that can confuse.

For you who are more adventuresome, there are other instruments for investing. Some are a higher risk than others, usually the higher the risk, the bigger the return. In this short dissertation my only concern is to suggest how you might keep your savings safe. There is no magic to absolute safety except to buy gold and bury it in your back yard. A last word about money and taxes, the Government can not give to anyone that it does not take away from someone else.

44
Shut Your Mouth

Finally ER-AH has been replaced with some new expression, they are used primarily so the user can stall in the middle of a sentence and come up with more pointless words to end the sentence. Here are some ill-assorted expressions used in place of a meaningful vocabulary.

These are some of the most unloved words in the English language. These are just a few:

- Ya know
- How-ya-doin
- By and large
- Whatever
- Basically
- It is what it is
- Yada-yada
- My bad
- Awesome

45
Winning may not be Everything but Loosing is Nothing

I always looked upon selling as a contest. When I enter a contest I want to win. What other reason would you have to enter a contest? Either you win or you loose. If you win second place, you loose. If we can agree that winning is everything you and I are on the right track. I think about competitive sports among kids, a healthy thing, but telling them that loosing is okay is a mockery to their self esteem. You are saying to them it is okay to not win, but why in hell bother to enter a contest unless you want to win. Kids need to learn the lesson of winning and loosing, there is nothing in-between. The winners feel good and the losers don't. It prepares you for triumph and failure. We all have to learn to deal with both…that's life.

What makes a winner? It starts with a dream of something you want to become or something you wish to possess. What do you dream about? The things I dreamed about I had to go out and sell something first before I could have them. Before you launched yourself into adulthood, you do your utmost to learn all you can about what you want to do with the rest of your life. You see an objective and begin to chart your course to get there. To people in overdrive, don't let failures along the way get in your way. Look around you. There are winners and losers all over the place. The winners are achievers. They have learned how to use precious time to the best advantage. They stay focused.

How do you get into the winning mind-set? The dreams you have are the engine to successfully keep you marching toward your target that looms out there on the horizon. Along the way you will find rewarding events that reinforce your strength. They are the goodies that make your voyage worthwhile. You might be wondering what I am talking about, but it's the simple things that matter. Example: knowledge, no matter how you get it. Next: a home, spouse and children where love, trust and togetherness are shared. All these things enrich the journey and the economic environment you have chosen and are compatible with the life style you have selected. Theoretically with all the above stuff you are comfortable, but winning the race is still the goal. The starters pistol went bang a good while ago for you, but you can go back to the starting line again and run a different race, that is, change jobs or your occupation only if your brain has the new equipment to handle it.

There is a price we all must pay to win. It's not the lottery, it is what you know and what you speculate that you think you know. It is learned by the observant, the reader, the scholar and staying with your dreams as a train travels down the tracks or a ship that stays the course. I am saying you may miss a lot of TV or golf games or other stuff because you are doing the productive activities to reach your dreams and your goals. Determination is not calculated by what you do when you feel like it, but what you do when you don't feel like it.

Perhaps you are a person who has already arrived at the reality of your dream, such as a tenured professor or the CEO of the company or having earned and saved enough money to be happily retired...well. Now is the time to extend your hand to help to the other climbers.

All in all, what is this thing called winning? Rarely will you win without tenacity. Follow diligently your dreams and the road map you have planned for yourself. Winning is, striving to obtain that which only one person in the race can obtain. No detours. No shortcuts. No kidding.

46
What Do You Want on Your Tombstone?

One of the most clever advertisements I recall was a billboard with only eight words, it said "WHAT DO YOU WANT ON YOUR TOMBSTONE". After driving past this sign for several weeks I was surprised to see it replaced with the same eight words, plus a picture of a mouth watering Pizza pie and the words "Extra Cheese or Pepperoni?" It was announcing a new frozen pizza named Tombstone and you could buy it in your local supermarket. It got your attention because it was provocative. It was clever marketing you couldn't forget. What do you want on your TOMBSTONE? Make mine pepperoni.

47
Inventions that Give and Take

I must admit that I am overwhelmed by the number of gadgets, devices and gizmos you can buy today that keep you in touch with everything. Most of them fit in your pocket or purse. They sing, buzz, ring, vibrate and play music. They all have screens that display everything from text messages to photographs of near and far flung places. They take and send pictures. They remind you of birthdays and dates you need to remember. They are wonderful toys for most and an important tool for others. It all depends on how you use them, some will waste your time and some people think they can't live without them. Business people find them indispensable. They make a lot of money for the makers and fees you pay for airtime. There is just one thing they can't do and that is replace that brain you have between your ears. You will admit that thinking is quite important if you are in sales and breathing. Time is all you have in your busy day and to waste it, is abusing a most valuable resource. In business, cell phones with a camera and laptops are indispensable. We used laptops for presentations, instruction and record keeping, plus more things to help sales people stay engaged and focused. Although this may sound like I'm knocking these marvelous products, that is not true, all I am saying is that the way we use them can make them a thief of time. It is the old story, your choices can make or break you.

48
Is Your Life Structured?

I am a list person. When I have many tasks before me, I make a list so I don't forget stuff. Perhaps we are products of how we were raised by our parents. My Dad's job for most of his life was managing a factory that made cutlery, scissors and other cutting devises. He always carried 3x5 inch cards in his shirt pocket where he wrote what he had to do or procure for the factory. While talking to his foremen he also took notes on what he needed to do when he returned to his office. That's where I got into the habit of lists. If I have to go to the supermarket I make a list. When I operated the photographic studio, I kept a to-do list on my desk. If you don't make lists you are either unemployed or have an extra good memory. It doesn't matter where or how you keep your lists just as long as you keep one. It is a way of keeping things in your life shipshape. It is never too late to start. There is paper and pen by my bed, in the den, bath room, kitchen and my car. I like things tidy and I hope you do too.

49
Old Charlie and His Hammer

It was a revolutionary new product and would soon be used in all automobiles. It was "Safety Glass". At the first sales meeting everyone wanted to know how old Charley had the best sales record that year selling safety glass. He said he put a piece of glass on the buyer's desk and smacked it with a hammer (when it broke, it didn't shatter). All the salesmen took his suggestion. At the next sales meeting, Old Charley had the best sales records again. How did you do it they all wanted to know? He said he put the glass on the buyer's desk and gave the hammer to the buyer and said, "you try it". Whatever Charley did at the third sales meeting has not been revealed to me but by getting your customer involved in some way is good business. When I sold color postcards I would hand my prospect a handful of postcards and let him shuffle through at his own speed. Now, two people are involved in the selling process instead of one. Try it.

50
Making Connections

Someone told me that when you cast your bread on the water, it all comes back to you in wonderful ways you'd never expect. That is why I try to give my fellow sales friends tips and leads that might help them. If you do this you might find that "Do unto others as you would have them do unto you" works, also by helping a customer find sources they need which you can't fulfill goes a long way to keep relationships healthy.

Way back when my sales efforts were solely in the state where I lived, there was a group I was able to join. We had monthly gatherings of fifty or so. There was always a time before lunch where we would take turns and talk about a lead pursuant to something we had heard, seen or had helpful information that would assist one of us find new business. There was always good humor and kidding going on but the networking we did helped us all at one time or another. We just had one rule. No two businesses of the same type could belong, only one of a kind. When my business needed to draw upon a much larger territory than the northern part of New Jersey the group no longer served my purpose and I quietly resigned, however I can assure you another photographer was ready to take my place. Networking works, but you need to remember to return the favor. It's a two way street.

51
You Can Learn from Squirrels

A friend of mine told me this story. His wife put an empty plastic peanut butter jar in the recycle bin by their back door. An hour or so later she saw a squirrel appear to be playing with it in the yard. On closer observation she noticed the squirrel was attempting to remove the lid. When that didn't work he started to chew off the cap but soon gave up. Afterward she went out in the yard and returned the jar to the recycle bin. The next day Mr. Squirrel had the peanut butter jar out of the bin and again attempted to chew off the lid and again it was to no avail. Later that day she put the jar back in the recycle bin. The third day the squirrel was back and so was the peanut butter jar. He was holding it firmly in his small paws and chewing away at the opposite end. The plastic being quite thin at this part, the squirrel was making good progress and was soon able to get at the left over peanut butter, almost out loud she said "bravo" because the squirrel had succeeded and was rewarded with the left-overs the family could not get out of the jar.

All this goes to prove that persistence pays off even if it is only a little peanut butter. When you add and apply persistence as permanent sales tools in your kit, you also get rewards. It applies to other things in your ever present job of obtaining business. For instance it applies to follow-up calls and introducing new products to squirrels and customers. You must also be persistent in advertising and repeat mailings to keep you and your firms name ever present before customers and those who are yet to become customers.

52
This is for Free, Will You Buy It?

Nobody in your life really cares about your over-all health except those who depend on you for their well being. If you get sick you will get three things: real love, sham love and medical bills some of which your health insurance won't pay. Health care is expensive and the sicker you are the more you cost to maintain or repair. So, don't get sick. You can start your plan to not get sick by understanding about the choices you make are reflected by your life style, but you are saying to me there are exceptions, I'm not denying you are right, but all the exceptions you can think of are not a consideration now.

We have talked about this before, it bears repitition. You can start your reformation by adopting this slogan; "MODERATION IN ALL THINGS". Your ultimate goal is to be your personal best. As basic as this may seem, to be your best you need enough sleep, eat healthy food, get some exercise and possess a loving and understanding nature. Does this mean that you need to be told not to eat junk food, drink booze to excess, when to go to bed at night or to let the daily news warp your brain? The answer to this is NO. Ideally you return to the watchwords "Moderation in all things". Keep your body in good condition it is the apparatus that makes everything you are work. If you do this, you will find that the things that hem you in on a daily basis can be dealt with more effectively. We all veer off course from time to time and that is certainly understandable so long as we get back on track sooner rather than later. Life may not always give you everything you want but it will usually give you everything you need.

One last word on this matter of moderation, if you are a mountain climber, race car driver, parachute jumper or do other activities that involve your physical safety you are a risk taker of the highest order.

Don't play the fools game. (Business is also risky, but the good thing is you usually live to play the game another day.) The sensation or "rush" from this is supposed to be the reward. You win if you don't die. Over confidence and lack of planning causes most of the accidents or death from these activities. Skill, mental and physical strength help the daredevil escape until as the old man on the mountain says you use up the odds one degree too far. The traits of these extremists are conceit, pride and vanity, one or all play a major part in the reason people keep trying to prove themselves in this manner. Don't get trapped in the never ending merry-go-round. Remember Goldilocks never returned to the Three Bears.

53
A Last Word from the Old Man on the Mountain

When the merchant ships of old left port, the people on shore would speculate how long they might be gone and if they would return. Most came back with rich cargoes and lived good lives, but some were lost at sea because of storms, lack of seamanship or worst of all pirates. In your life, storms will come and go and the pirates will try to get you. Be the master of your ship. It will be your job to not only get accurate weather reports of what the future holds, but to understand there will be risk and you'll get bruised, but stay informed and hold your course. Do this and success will follow you through the ups and downs of business and your personal life. God Bless and Good Luck.